A LITTLE
SCOTTISH
CASTLES

By
Charles Maclean
Illustrated by
Sheila Maclean

First published in 1995 by
The Appletree Press Ltd
19–21 Alfred Street, Belfast BT2 8DL
Tel. +44 (0) 1232 243074 Fax. +44 (0) 1232 246756
Copyright © The Appletree Press Ltd, 1995
Printed in the UAE. All rights reserved.
No part of this publication may be reproduced or
transmitted in any form or by any means, electronic
or mechanical, photocopying, recording or in any
information or retrieval system without prior
permission in writing from the publisher.

A Little Book of Scottish Castles

A catalogue record for this book is available
from the British Library.

ISBN 0-86281-546-0

9 8 7 6 5 4 3 2

For Simon Miller, 'The Captain of Cleish', and
Sir Lachlan Maclean of Duart and Morvern –
both well worthy of their castles.

Contents

Introduction

There are at least 1,500 castles in Scotland, possibly twice that number, depending upon your definition of what constitutes a "castle".

During the Iron Age, people began to build fortifications on hill-tops, with concentric ditches and earthworks surrounding stone ramparts, topped by a wooden stockade. Whole communities were safe within such structures. Later, similar but smaller forts were built – *duns* – large enough to protect a family or a chieftain's household. Then, between about 100 B.C. and 100 A.D., formidable cylindrical towers were built, usually with outer defences creating a courtyard or *barmkin* which provided security for lesser buildings. These *brochs* are unique to Scotland and display remarkable ingenuity and a high level of technology.

The feudalisation of Scotland along Anglo-Norman lines began in the early twelfth century, and purists define this as the commencement of true castle building. The word "castel" first appears shortly before the Norman Conquest to describe the "motte and bailey" forts erected by Norman knights in England. The earliest stone castles were merely high walls protecting the buildings within, usually taking advantage of natural defences. These are known as castles of *enceinte* (enclosure).

The Crusades introduced the West to Byzantine fortresses, which were greatly superior to European fortifications. Corner towers were attached to the curtain wall, machicolations were introduced along the wall-head, a second and third line of defence within the castle was considered desirable, and beyond this was erected a *donjon* or *keep*. Later, the major defences were moved to the castle's most vulnerable point, its entrance.

Building vertically has always appealed to the Scots' imagination, and many hundreds of tower houses were erected in Scotland between the fourteenth and seventeenth centuries. Early examples were simple cubes with thick walls and crenellated parapets, open-roofed turrets and four or five floors. Unlike English keeps, they had no forebuilding, were not surrounded by strong outer walls – although most had barmkins – and relied for their outer defence on ramparts, moats and ditches.

In 1535 legislation required landowners to build "a sufficient Barmekin" of stone and lime, with "a tour in the samen for himsel". The need for a secure and defensible residence was still very real in Scotland – the Wars of Religion, the Civil War, the constant threat from bands of lawless and landless gypsies and from clan raids, all encouraged the building of fortified houses. But this was also the period of the Renaissance: owners sought comfort and prestige as well as security, and Scottish architects made an exuberant and unique contribution to European architecture.

The castles I have chosen exemplify most periods and styles of castle building in Scotland. Inclusion has been based on historical and architectural importance, visual appeal and with a view to providing a reasonable geographical spread. All are easily accessible and open to the public.

Charles MacLean
Edinburgh, February 1995

5

Balvenie

Balvenie was the chief seat of the powerful Comyn family, Earls of Buchan, until their eclipse by Robert the Bruce in 1308. Their fortress consisted of a high *enceinte* wall (mostly still standing) enclosing a quadrangle 160 feet by 130 feet, with towers on two corners, all surrounded by a wide ditch.

Following the fall of the Comyns, the lordship of Balvenie passed to Bruce's most ardent supporters, the "Black" Douglases, but they fell out with, and were ultimately overthrown by, King James II in 1455. Their estates were forfeited to the Crown, and Balvenie was granted to John Stewart, later Earl of Atholl, upon payment of a red rose annually. The Stewart Earls of Atholl retained the castle until the seventeenth century, and most of what remains today was constructed by them. Domestic buildings were built along the east front of the castle, with windows piercing the curtain wall. Then, in the mid-sixteenth century, a tall L-plan tower was built at the eastern angle of the curtain wall, with a large circular tower projecting beyond the corner itself and two smaller towers facing into the courtyard.

By the time Mary, Queen of Scots stayed at Balvenie in 1562, the grim fortress had been transformed into a Renaissance mansion – still capable of vigorous defence with window grills and ground-floor gun loops – but with the air of an elegant and sophisticated country house.

Bothwell

Lanark (Strathclyde Region)

Bothwell Castle was built in the mid-thirteenth century on a rocky outcrop overlooking the Clyde near Lanark. Its builder was Sir Walter de Moravia, co-Regent of Scotland in 1255, who had acquired the barony of Bothwell through marriage to an Oliphant heiress. Its design was influenced by Coucy-le-Château at Aisne, France (which was considered one of the grandest military structures in Europe) and had a massive circular donjon – 90-feet high, with walls 15-feet thick – as its key feature. Behind the great tower is a bailey surrounded by high walls and protected by a further two towers – one round, the other square – at its corners. A curtain wall was planned, but never completed.

Sir Andrew Murray, third Lord of Bothwell, led the Scots against the English in 1297, and was mortally wounded at Stirling Bridge. His castle was taken by Edward I, and in 1298–99 William Wallace, who had succeeded Murray as leader of the Scots, besieged it for fourteen months. The mighty donjon was so badly damaged during the Wars of Independence that it was never fully repaired. By the 1330s, it was again in English hands: Edward III made Bothwell his headquarters for a month or so in 1336. When Sir Andrew Murray recaptured it the following year he slighted it and for twenty years it lay derelict. In 1360 the lordship of Bothwell passed through marriage to "Black Archibald the Grim", third Earl of Douglas and Lord of Galloway, who largely rebuilt and held Bothwell until it was forfeited in 1445.

Caerlaverock

Near Dumfries (Dumfries & Galloway Region)

Caerlaverock stands seven miles south-east of Dumfries, surrounded by a moat in what was once extensive marshland. It is among the finest examples of baronial architecture in Scotland, and is unique as a triangular *enceinte* castle.

It was built between 1290 and 1300 by Sir Herbert de Maxwell, on the site of an earlier castle, probably as a defence against sea-borne English invaders. Improvements, such as machicolations, gun loops and a splendid neo-classical mansion, were added right up to the seventeenth century.

Caerlaverock has round towers on two angles – one of them is ruinous; the other is known as Murdoch's Tower, after Murdoch, Duke of Albany, who was imprisoned here for high treason in 1424. On the third angle is a massive gate-house, considered to be the best in Scotland, with twin drum towers and room for a portcullis and drawbridge machinery.

The castle was besieged and captured at least five times during its history. It fell first in 1300 to Edward I, then was recaptured and partially destroyed by the Scots. By 1356 it was again in English hands for a short period, and again during Henry VIII's "Rough Wooing" of Mary, Queen of Scots in 1545. In 1570, it was bombarded into submission by the Earl of Sussex's artillery, and finally it was taken after a lengthy siege by a Covenanting army in 1640. This ended Caerlaverock's life as a habitable residence.

Campbell

The castle stands on a spur of the Ochil Hills high above the town of Dollar, with steep wooded ravines on either side, and offers stupendous views. History does not relate who built the first tower here, nor why it was originally called Castle Gloom, with the burns of Care and of Sorrow on either side. Even the name Dollar comes from *dolour*, meaning sadness.

In 1493, it was acquired by Colin Campbell, first Earl of Argyll and Chancellor of Scotland. He had its name changed to Castle Campbell by an Act of Parliament in 1489 and added a spacious range of buildings on the north side of the courtyard.

Further buildings were added by his successors in the sixteenth and early seventeenth centuries, including a handsome Renaissance-style arched loggia. John Knox, the ardent Protestant reformer, preached at the castle in 1556 on a grassy slope, now known as "Knox's Pulpit".

In 1645, Montrose's army attempted to take the castle, spurred on by a regiment of Macleans, sworn enemies of the Campbells, who wanted an excuse to burn it. Nine years later General Monck succeeded in storming it and did much damage.

Cawdor

Near Nairn (Highland Region)

The early Thanes of Cawdor were Calders and held large estates around Inverness from at least the fourteenth century. They built their substantial keep six miles south of Nairn in 1454, after the Thane of the day was instructed in a dream to load a donkey with gold and to build wherever it came to rest. The donkey stopped under a Hawthorn, or May Tree, which can be seen to this day preserved inside the castle.

The Calder line came to an end when Archibald Campbell, Earl of Argyll, resolved to marry his son to the infant female heir, Muriel. After much bloodshed, he captured the child and raised her in his castle of Inveraray. Thereafter the Campbells became the Barons and, later, Earls of Cawdor. The present Earl still lives in Cawdor Castle – the only private castle in Scotland with its own drawbridge!

The original building was a plain tower, with bartizans on the corners, surrounded by a deep ditch and reached via a drawbridge and moveable timber stair to the first floor. A curtain wall was added in 1500, and during the following century the north and west wings were enlarged to form a courtyard to the north of the keep.

The castle contains several impressive Renaissance fireplaces, the most curious of which dates from 1511 and commemorates the marriage of Sir John Campbell to Muriel Calder. It depicts a fox smoking a pipe. Yet the first record of tobacco in Europe was not until 1558, when Philip II of Spain was presented with a plant!

Claypotts

Broughty Ferry, Dundee, Angus (Tayside Region)

It has been said that Claypotts looks like an architectural exercise to incorporate as many improbable features and unusual angles within as small a compass as possible. The main block is oblong, with two stout circular towers on opposite corners (making the plan Z-shaped). These towers are surmounted by rectangular garrets with crow-stepped gables and floors corbelled out over the cylindrical tower, so that they look like elevated cottages. One tower was built twenty years after the other. There are also two smaller, D-shaped towers in the angles, housing staircases. The walls are well provided with gun loops and shot holes – and the plan of the castle permits all-round defence, with the round towers providing covering fire for the central block – although, in fact, Claypotts never witnessed violent action.

The castle was built by John Strachan, though the land belonged to the Abbey of Lindores in Fife. It was later sold to Sir William Graham of Claverhouse, grandfather of the famous "Bloody Claver'se", Viscount Dundee, who led the Jacobite army in the rising of 1689 and died at the moment of his victory at Killiecrankie in 1690. His lands were then forfeited, and in 1694 Claypotts passed to the Earl of Angus, through whose descendants it came to the Earls of Home. It was never lived in by its owners but was used as lodgings for farm labourers in the nineteenth century before passing to the State in 1926. Unfortunately, it is now closely hemmed in by busy roads and housing estates.

Craigmillar

Edinburgh, Midlothian (Lothian Region)

Craigmillar stands on a small hill on the southern outskirts of Edinburgh, and commands excellent views in all directions. It is likely that an early fortress made use of the splendid site, but the present castle dates from 1374.

The well-preserved L-plan keep is the earliest part of the existing building and was raised by Sir Simon Preston of Garton. In 1427, a 30-foot high, heavily machicolated curtain wall with angle towers was built round it – the best preserved example of its kind in Scotland. Early in the sixteenth century a wide outer courtyard was added.

James III imprisoned his younger brother at Craigmillar under suspicion of treason and in 1563 Mary, Queen of Scots received the English ambassador here and was told that if she wished to remain on friendly terms with her cousin, Queen Elizabeth I, she must find an acceptable husband. Queen Mary was a frequent visitor to the castle, and it was here that the famous pact – known as the Craigmillar Bond – to murder her husband, Lord Darnley was drawn up by some of her leading nobles.

The Preston family sold the estate to Sir John Gilmour, Lord President of the Court of Session, in 1660. The Gilmours moved out of the castle in the eighteenth century, and by 1775 it was a romantic ruin. There was a proposal in 1842 to restore it as a Scottish residence for Queen Victoria, but this plan came to nothing, and the family placed the castle under the guardianship of the State in 1946.

Crathes

Banchory, Aberdeenshire (Grampian Region)

Building commenced at Crathes in 1553 – a time when the
need for defence was beginning to give way to demands for
comfort and style – and the castle took forty-three years to
complete. It has been continuously inhabited since, and is an
outstanding example of an L-plan tower house. It was built
by the Burnetts of Leys, who had been given the land by
Robert the Bruce in return for services during the Wars of
Independence. Alexander Burnet began the tower but it was
completed by his great-grandson family arms and
monograms decorate the wall above the entrance.

The lower storeys are plain (the mock-Renaissance first-
floor window was added in Victorian times) but the upper
works incorporate an exuberant variety of corbelling,
bartizans (both square and circular), stair turrets, mouldings
and gargoyles. The tower has rounded corners and tapers
towards the top. In medieval castle design, this was so that
it was more difficult to dislodge corner stones and weaken
the structure, and so that enemies could not hide beneath the
battlements and mine the foundations, but at Crathes the
features are clearly adopted for aesthetic reasons.

Not all are: the traditional *yett* (gate) is for rear defence,
as is an awkwardly placed "tripping-stone" at the top of the
turnpike staircase. The upper rooms have beautifully painted
ceilings and the magnificent eighteenth century gardens,
with 200-year-old yew hedges and even older lime avenues,
contain many rare plants.

Crichton

Crichton, near Pathhead, Midlothian (Lothian Region)

Standing amid rolling countryside above the River Tyne, not far from Edinburgh, Crichton was originally a three-storey tower house and barmkin, built in the late thirteenth century by one John de Crichton. His son William was elevated to the peerage and became Lord Chancellor of Scotland in 1439. He added a large oblong keep-gatehouse to the tower on the south side, as befitted his rank and power, with spacious and well-lit halls on the first and second floors.

In the late fifteenth century a three-floor west wing was added, with a six-storey round tower at the south-west angle, and a century later the courtyard was completed by the addition of a residential block on the north side. By this time, though, the Crichtons had lost their estates for treasonable activities and their lands passed to the Hepburn Earls of Bothwell. James, the fourth Earl, was Mary, Queen of Scots lover, and after his forfeiture, James VI gave both Crichton Castle and the Bothwell earldom to Francis Stewart (1576).

Stewart was a ruffian, but was well travelled and had extremely good taste. He resolved to transform his castle into a Renaissance palace, and the most obvious evidence of his work is the north façade, which has an eight bay arcade at ground level, and is clad with diamond-patterned stones, all in the Italianate manner. The effect is most striking, especially on a sunny day when the whole façade is patterned with sharp angular shadows.

Dirleton

Dirleton, East Lothian (Lothian Region)

Set upon a rocky knoll on the edge of one of the prettiest villages in Scotland, Dirleton Castle was built in the mid-1200s by John de Vaux, steward to Marie de Coucy, who had married King Alexander II in 1239. It was built in the fashion of the famous Château-le-Coucy in Normandy, with a massive drum tower or *donjon* as its key feature. A further three towers (one is now demolished) created a tight triangular courtyard and provided stout defences for the castle entrance. The whole was surrounded by a deep moat, at least fifty feet wide, spanned by a moveable wooden bridge and drawbridge. In 1298 it fell to the warrior Bishop of Durham, Anthony Beck, who used battering rams and siege-machinery to force the defendants into submission.

The barony of Dirleton was acquired by the Halyburton family during the next century, and they rebuilt much of the castle, extended the accommodation and added gun platforms. In 1515 it passed to the Ruthven family, Earls of Gowrie, who "modernised" it by adding a comfortable three-storey residence and creating a formal garden and bowling green below the castle walls. It was described by a contemporary as "the pleasantest dwelling in Scotland".

Dirleton was besieged for the last time in 1650, by Cromwell's army under General Monck. This time the besiegers had mortars, the fourth shot from which smashed the draw-bridge and doorway. The garrison of irregular moss-troopers surrendered immediately.

Doune

Doune, Stirlingshire (Central Region)

Doune stands on a narrow isthmus, high above the River Teith, on the outskirts of the town of Doune, just north of Stirling. The district was formerly the important earldom of Menteith, and the man who built the castle was Robert Stewart, Earl of Menteith and Fife, Duke of Albany (after 1398), and younger son of King Robert II.

Albany was a hard and ambitious man. He had been Governor of the Kingdom for the last two years of his father's life, and when this position was given to his nephew, had him starved to death at Falkland. He resumed the Regency upon his brother, Robert III's, death in 1406, and held it until he died in 1420.

Doune Castle was built shortly before 1400. Its arrangement demonstrates the fears that beset powerful men in an age of "horrible destructions, burnings and slaughter": the Duke's quarters are in the five-storey high gate-house tower, which controlled the portcullis and entry to the castle, and his chambers were not even accessible from the adjacent Great Hall and the guest tower beyond it. The buildings were secured from behind by a 40-foot high curtain wall, complete with corbelled turrets on its corners.

Murdoch, second Duke of Albany, was executed by James I in 1424, and Doune then became a royal residence, frequently used as a hunting lodge. During 1745 it was taken by the Jacobites and used as a prison, under the command of a nephew of Rob Roy.

Duart

Isle of Mull (Strathclyde Region)

Duart has been the seat of the High Chiefs of Clan Maclean since the fourteenth century. Its massive keep – which rises nearly 40 feet and has walls 10-feet thick in places – was built by Lachlan "Lubanach" (The Crafty) Maclean in about 1390, within a vast curtain wall which is probably a century older. The whole edifice stands dramatically on a cliff-edge overlooking the Sound of Mull: Duart comes from the gaelic *dubh-ard* meaning "the dark headland".

Crafty Lachlan made his fortune by kidnapping the first Lord of the Isles and forcing him to grant "wide lands" in Mull and the hand of his daughter in marriage.

The zenith of Maclean power was in the late sixteenth century, and the castle was added to and domestically improved during this period and again in the 1630s. During the civil wars of the seventeenth century, the Macleans supported the royalist cause and when King James VII went into exile in 1689 the Maclean lands, including Duart Castle, were seized by the Earl of Argyll. The chiefs went into exile, while the badly damaged castle was garrisoned by government troops until 1751 and then abandoned.

In 1911 the ruin was bought back and sensitively restored by Colonel Sir Fitzroy Maclean. It is now the home of his great-grandson, Sir Lachlan Maclean, twenty-eighth Chief of Clan Gillean.

Dunnottar

Stonehaven, Aberdeenshire

Dunnottar stands on an island, connected to the mainland only by a narrow isthmus, with sheer, 160-feet cliffs on every side, except for a little gully on the landward side which is the only point of access. The top of the island – some 3.5 acres in extent – is flat and verdant. The isthmus is a narrow ridge of inaccessible cliff, but, for added security, even this has been cut through so as to sever all connection with the mainland. A Pictish fort once occupied the summit of the rock, and St Ninian established a church there in the fifth century, within which William Wallace incinerated the rock's English garrison in 1297.

The first proper castle (the existing L-plan keep) was built at Dunnottar in 1382 by Sir William Keith, Great Marischal of Scotland – for which he was excommunicated, since the church regarded the entire rock as hallowed ground. Between about 1540 and 1650 many further buildings were erected on the rock – formidable defensive works around the entrance, extensive domestic buildings, stables, smithy, stores and a chapel.

Charles II was welcomed here from France on his way south in 1650 and left his private papers and valuables there. Following his defeat at Worcester the next year, the Regalia were also brought to Dunnottar. As a result the castle was besieged for eight months; by the time the small garrison was forced to capitulate, the Regalia had been smuggled out and hidden in a church nearby.

Dunstaffnage

Dunbeg, near Oban, Argyll (Strathclyde Region)

The strategic importance of Dunstaffnage's position has been apparent since ancient times. The huge lump of conglomerate rock upon which it stands is a natural fortress, and there is a plausible tradition that it was the capital of the kingdom of Dalriada in the seventh century.

The present curtain wall, 60-feet high in places, was raised in the mid-thirteenth century by Ewen MacDougall of Argyll. His son, Alasdair of Argyll married a sister of the "Black Comyn", whose son was murdered by Robert the Bruce. So, inevitably, MacDougall supported the unsuccessful faction during the Wars of Independence, and suffered accordingly. Bruce took Dunstaffnage, effected repairs and installed a royal garrison. It was garrisoned 350 years later by Cromwellian and government troops, as it was during both the 1715 and 1745 Jacobite risings. Flora MacDonald who had aided Bonnie Prince Charlie in 1746, was held here en route to the Tower of London.

About 1550 Dunstaffnage came into the hands of the Campbell Earls of Argyll, who appointed an hereditary "captain" to hold it on their behalf. Early captains altered the entrance to the castle and constructed a gate-house, and in the sixteenth century the upper storeys of this and other domestic buildings within the curtain wall were made more comfortable. In 1725 a two-storey house was built at the north-east end of the courtyard. The current Captain of Dunstaffnage is the twenty-second to hold that position.

Dunvegan

Isle of Skye (Highland Region)

Standing on a headland in the north-west of Skye, Dunvegan is one of the few castles in Scotland which has housed the same family – the Macleods of Dunvegan, high chiefs of Clan Macleod – since its foundation in about 1200. Twenty-one generations of chiefs have lived here, many of whom are commemorated in the magnificent collection of family portraits which hangs in the castle.

The first castle was built by Leod, name-father of the clan, who acquired the whole of Skye through marriage to the daughter of the Norse Seneschal of the northern isles. As was typical of island castles of this date, Dunvegan began as a huge curtain wall surmounting an easily defended rock promontory, above a sheltered sea loch. Until the eighteenth century its only entrance was by a sea gate on the north side, and the landward side was protected by a fosse 60-feet wide.

The three-storey square keep on the north-west angle dates from the fourteenth century and the small turrets and high flag tower, known as the Fairy Tower, were added 200 years later. Much of the rest of the building dates from the 1840s, when the castle was extended and remodelled in the Picturesque-style.

Dunvegan houses many historical relics and treasures, including the famous Fairy Flag, a silken banner made in the Middle East over 1000 years ago and possibly brought back from Constantinople by King Harald Haardrade of Norway, who was defeated at Stamford Bridge in 1066.

Edinburgh

Midlothian (Lothian and Borders Region)

There was a prehistoric fortress on the summit of the extinct volcano which dominates the skyline of Scotland's capital city, but the earliest existing building, Queen Margaret's Chapel, dates from the eleventh century. The present castle broadly follows the plan devised by David II in the 1360s, but little of the medieval building survives. The site has been a victim of its own importance: successive owners have been more concerned with its defensibility and military uses than with preserving antiquities.

The castle was "slighted" by Robert the Bruce in 1313, then David II re-fortified it and built a large tower-house on the site of what is now the Half-Moon Battery. James I built a palace adjacent to David's Tower in the early 1400s and this was extensively rebuilt by James IV. The Great Hall was the meeting chamber of the Scottish Parliament until 1639: the earlier hall was the scene of the infamous Black Dinner in 1440, when the youthful Earl of Douglas and his younger brother were murdered in the presence of the eight-year-old King James II.

The residential part of the castle was again altered by Mary, Queen of Scots in 1566: the small room in which she gave birth to James VI (James I of England) is shown to visitors, and nearby the ancient and magnificent Regalia of Scotland (the Crown Jewels) are displayed. Among the more recent buildings that make up the castle complex are the Scottish National War Memorial, the Regimental Museum of the Royal Scots (the oldest infantry regiment in the British army) and the Scottish United Services Museum (opened 1931).

Edzell

Edzell, in the foothills of the Grampian Mountains at the mouth of Glenesk, was the ancient seat of the Lindsays, Earls of Crawford. It was acquired by them in 1358 through marriage to a Stirling heiress, and the first castle at Edzell was built by the Stirlings. This was replaced by a tower house in the early sixteenth century, to which was added, in 1580, a mansion which has been described as "one of the noblest of Scottish baronial edifices", although it is now ruinous. Nine years later King James VI received the submission of the Earl of Errol at Edzell, where he was a guest of its owner, Sir David Lindsay.

In 1604, Sir David designed and built a walled "pleasance", known as "The Garden of the Zodiac", which he decorated with heraldic and symbolic sculptures. It is the finest of its kind in Scotland. Adjacent to the garden is a two-storey summer-house and a bath-house.

Edzell has had a number of distinguished visitors. Mary, Queen of Scots held a Privy Council here in 1562 and stayed at the castle; Cromwell garrisoned it in 1651. Sadly, the Lindsays had to sell their castle and Inveresk in 1715 to pay off huge debts. The castle changed hands several times, but in 1746 was vandalised, apparently by unpaid local creditors.

39

Eilean Donan

Loch Duich, Kintail (Highland Region)

Eilean Donan, a small island at the mouth of Loch Duich, near Kyle of Lochalsh, has one of the most picturesque settings of any Scottish castle. There was a Pictish fort here once, and later a Celtic Saint – Donan, after whom the island is named – took up solitary residence. King Alexander II raised strong walls on the island in 1220, as a defence against Viking invaders, while the square keep at the north-east angle was added in the fourteenth century.

The castle was the chief stronghold in the west of the powerful Clan MacKenzie, and was held for them by their loyal cadets, the MacRaes, who became known as "MacKenzie's shirt of mail". On one occasion in 1539, when the castle was being besieged from the sea by Donald "Gorm" MacDonald of Sleat, disaster was only averted by Duncan MacRae shooting Sleat in the foot with an arrow – he bled to death from the wound.

During the Jacobite rising of 1719, William MacKenzie, fifth Earl of Seaforth, garrisoned Eilean Donan with Spanish troops, and as a result it was besieged by three Royal Navy frigates. Its ancient walls were breached with the first broadsides, and the castle was abandoned. It remained ruinous until 1932 when it was restored and extensively rebuilt by Colonel John MacRae-Gilstrap, to be the seat of the MacRae chiefs and to house the Clan MacRae War Memorial. The bridge which connects it to the mainland was added at this time.

Fraser

Kemnay, Aberdeenshire (Grampian Region)

The name Fraser first appears in Scottish records in the mid-twelfth century – it is of French origin, and may derive from *fraise* "strawberry", the leaves of which appear in the Fraser arms. One Thomas Fraser exchanged lands in Stirlingshire for Muchal-in-Mar, Aberdeenshire, in the mid-fifteenth century and is thought to have built a castle on the site of the present Castle Fraser.

The castle as it stands today was begun by the fifth laird and completed by his son. The central block of the house is a four-storey, double-width tower house. In 1592 a massive drum tower, rising a further two storeys, was added to one corner, and a square tower to the corner diagonally opposite, completing the Z-plan. Two lengthy wings were added in 1614, creating a courtyard, entered by an arched gateway flanked by lodges. The walls throughout are liberally provided with gun loops and shot holes.

The sixth laird, Andrew Fraser, was created Lord Fraser in 1633. The second Lord Fraser was a staunch Covenanter, and Montrose ravaged his lands, but not his castle. The fourth, and last, Lord Fraser was a Jacobite and died when he fell off a cliff while fleeing from Government troops in 1716. The castle passed to a relative when the last Fraser died childless in 1897.

The castle remained empty until 1922 when it was bought by Viscount Cowdray. It was gifted to the National Trust for Scotland in 1976 by his daughter and her husband.

Fyvie

Fyvie, near Old Meldrum, Aberdeenshire
(Grampian Region)

There are five towers at Fyvie, each named for one of the families who have owned the castle since the fourteenth century. The original building on the site was a large twelfth century castle of *enceinte*. It was used as a royal hunting lodge until 1380, when Robert III gave it to his cousin, Sir James de Lindsay, it then passed to Lindsay's brother-in-law, Sir Henry Preston, in 1390. The Preston Tower, on the western end of the southern façade, is the oldest part of the existing mansion and is thought to incorporate the remains of the earlier castle.

The Meldrum tower was added at the eastern end of the façade in the fifteenth century and the whole south range was elegantly unified and embellished in about 1600 – not east by the addition of the Seton Towers. Sir Alexander Seton, later Lord Chancellor of Scotland and guardian of Charles I (who spent part of his childhood at Fyvie) was responsible for the improvement, and much of the baronial detail and sumptuous plasterwork is thanks to his good taste, and the patronage of King James VI.

The last private owner of Fyvie was the Leith family. Alexander Leith was a local man who made a fortune in the American steel industry and was created Lord Leith in 1905. He left a remarkable collection of paintings and other works of art and built the Leith Tower at the north-west corner of the castle.

Glamis

Glamis, by Forfar, Angus (Tayside Region)

At the core of Glamis Castle is a substantial L-plan tower, its summit exuberantly decorated with bartizans and gazebos, balustrades and battlements. The earliest part of this structure dates from the mid-fifteenth century (but probably incorporates an earlier tower), and was built by the first Lord Glamis, whose family – the Lyons – had been granted the lands in 1372.

As it stands today, the castle is largely the product of augmentation in about 1600 by Patrick Lyon, ninth Lord Glamis and first Earl of Kinghorne with great imaginative breadth and elaboration of detail. Such complexity of construction gives rise to many stories of walled-up chambers and secret passages. Once, when the laird was away, the staff hung sheets from every window of every room, yet from the outside they were still able to count several "unmarked" windows, which must belong to closed-up rooms.

Glamis is one of the most haunted houses in Scotland: it has a White Lady (supposedly Lady Jane Glamis, who was executed 1537); "Earl Beardie" (the fourth Earl of Crawford, who used to play cards with the first Lord Glamis); and the "Terrible Secret" – a monster, supposedly a deformed heir to the title who was immured.

Glamis is the seat of the Earls of Kinghorne and Strathmore, who still live there. It is the family home of Queen Elizabeth, The Queen Mother and both she and Princess Margaret were born here.

Hermitage

Hermitage is probably the most forbidding castle in all Scotland, and having been restored in the nineteenth century, it is in good order – externally, at least. It stands in desolate country at the head of Liddesdale, a district which was for several centuries disputed between the Scots and the English.

The original castle was built by the English Lord Dacre between 1338 and 1365. Then it belonged to Sir Nicholas de Saulis, Lord of Liddesdale, who strengthened it. De Saulis was notorious for his cruelty and met his end at a nearby stone circle called Nine Staine Rig, wrapped in lead and boiled alive by his long-suffering tenants.

In the 1370s the castle passed by marriage to the Douglases, who held it for a century, built a tall L-plan keep on the site and later strengthened it with massive corner towers. The east and west towers were joined by an immensely high gothic arch – a feature which combines with Hermitage's sheer walls and tiny windows to give a profound impression of grimness.

In 1566 Mary, Queen of Scots, rode to Hermitage from Jedburgh to comfort her lover, the Earl of Bothwell, who had been wounded in a skirmish with the Border reiver, "Little Jock" Elliott. The distance is twenty miles; she rode there and back in a day, in bad weather and while she was still recovering from the birth of her son. As a result she contracted pneumonia and almost died.

Huntingtower

Near Perth (Tayside Region)

Huntingtower was originally a plain tower called Ruthven Castle. Another tower was built alongside and connected to the first by a wooden bridge at parapet level, so that if one tower was taken by an enemy, the defenders could withdraw to the other. The gap was known as the "Maiden's Leap" because the laird's daughter leapt from one tower to the other to escape discovery in her lover's bedroom. The two towers were joined in the late seventeenth century.

In 1582, Ruthven's owner, the Earl of Gowrie, together with the Earls of Mar and Glencairn, kidnapped sixteen-year-old King James VI in an attempt to persuade him to dismiss his favourites. He was held prisoner in the castle for ten months while the rebellious earls ruled the country. When he escaped, Gowrie went to the scaffold. This event was known as "The Raid of Ruthven".

Eighteen years later King James had Gowrie's sons, the second Earl and the Master of Ruthven, murdered in their house in Perth, in a lurid adventure which has since baffled historians, as the only evidence was that of the king. There would, however, appear to be homosexual overtones to the case. The name "Ruthven" was then proscribed, and the castle, now known as Huntingtower, was taken into royal custody. Charles I later gave it to the father of Oliver Cromwell's reputed mistress, Betty Dysart.

Huntly

Huntly, Aberdeenshire (Grampian Region

The ruins of Castle Huntly stand above a rocky gorge, where the Rivers Deveron and Bogie meet, just outside the town of Huntly. The earliest castle here, known as Strathbogie, was a motte and bailey structure built by the Earl of Fife in the twelfth century. This was burned to the ground in 1452. The lands of Strathbogie were then transferred to Sir Adam Gordon of Huntly by Robert the Bruce.

The first Earl of Huntly was created in 1436, and he began to build a stone castle on the site in 1454: an oblong keep with a large circular tower in the south-west corner, surrounded by an extensive courtyard of secondary buildings. This was partially destroyed in 1594, but enough remained for the fifth Earl to add a splendid top storey, in the Renaissance style. He had spent some years in France (following his father's unsuccessful rebellion against Mary, Queen of Scots, and death at the Battle of Corrichie in 1562) and was much influenced by the new architectural fashions he saw there. When he returned to royal favour he was made a marquis in 1599. He embellished the main elevations of his castle with a handsome suite of oriel windows, an inscribed frieze and a magnificent heraldic main doorway.

The second Marquis was a fierce royalist during the civil war, and the King's representative in Scotland. His pride was such that he refused to co-operate with the great Montrose and was executed in 1649. The castle was badly damaged by Cromwellian troops, and has remained a roofless ruin ever since.

Tantallon

North Berwick, East Lothian (Lothian Region)

This huge, red sandstone castle stands on a promontory jutting out into the Firth of Forth, protected on its landward side by a great curtain wall, 50-feet high and 12-feet thick, beyond which there is a ditch and rampart. The wall is flanked by towers, and a massive gate-house keep juts out of the centre of the curtain and rises 30-feet above the wall-head.

There was a castle on the site before 1300, but the existing fortress – the last castle of *enceinte* to be raised in Scotland – was built for William, first Earl of Douglas, in 1350. Early in the following century a barbican was constructed in front of the gateway, and this was replaced in the 1530s by a forward tower, fitted with gun loops.

The Earls of Douglas were forfeited in 1455, and twenty-four years later James III gave Tantallon to another branch of this powerful family, Archibald "Bell-the-Cat" Douglas, fifth Earl of Angus. By 1491, Bell-the-Cat had fallen out with James' successor, and withstood a siege led by James IV in person. In 1528 this scene was re-enacted with different players – Archibald, sixth Earl of Angus and James V – but again Tantallon defeated the royal ordnance, the wily Earl even sallying forth to capture a number of cannons. Tantallon's final siege was in 1651, when it withstood General Monck's artillery for seventeen days, but by the end of this bombardment the flanking towers were in ruins and the accommodation uninhabitable.

Threave

Near Castle Douglas, Kirkcudbrightshire
(Dumfries and Galloway Region)

Threave was built in about 1370 by Archibald "the Grim", third Earl of Douglas and illegitimate son of "Good Sir James" Douglas, Robert the Bruce's companion-in-arms. The Douglases were Lords of Galloway, and Threave commanded their lands in the south-west.

The castle stands on an island in the River Dee, about a mile west of the town of Castle Douglas – a massive, five-storey keep, 75-feet high, with a curtain wall (now largely destroyed) and two flanking drum towers on each angle. Entrance was by a moveable wooden bridge between the first floor of the tower and a gate-house in the curtain wall. There was a ditch and rampart beyond the wall. The overall impression is dour and formidable. Archibald the Grim died in 1400, and by the middle of the century the mighty Douglases had over-reached themselves.

In 1552, William, the eighth Earl, was invited to dine with King James II at Stirling. A quarrel broke out, however, the king stabbed Douglas in the throat and a courtier split his head open with an axe. The ninth Earl took up arms against the Crown and one by one his castles were taken, until only Threave was left. The king went in person to supervise the siege, bringing with him some heavy bombards from Linlithgow, and the castle surrendered upon honourable terms. James II was later killed by one of his own cannon, while he was supervising the siege of Roxburgh.

Urquhart

Loch Ness, Inverness-shire (Highland Region)

Castle Urquhart occupies a sandstone promontory on the western shore of Loch Ness, and commands sweeping views up and down the loch. Its position was strategically important – it guards the entrance to the fertile Glen Urquhart, and the old road to Kyle of Lochalsh, Skye and the Hebrides.

There was a Pictish fort here in the sixth century, and by the twelfth century this had been replaced by a motte and bailey castle. The earliest remains visible today date from the thirteenth century, when Alan Durward, Justiciar of Scotland and first Lord Urquhart, built a keep on the lochside. Durward was accused of treason in 1252 and fled to England, when his castle was taken over by the Comyn family. This led to its being besieged and captured by Edward I in 1296. He ordered its fortifications to be enhanced, and it is possible that the gatehouse was built at this time.

During the fourteenth century the Macdonald Lords of the Isles pillaged Glen Urquhart four times and seized the castle; four times it was recaptured and patched up.

Urquhart is one of the largest castles in Scotland, but it is intrinsically weak on the landward side (its peninsula is lower than the surrounding country, so the castle was easily bombarded) and throughout its history it was repeatedly besieged, captured, destroyed and rebuilt. By the seventeenth century, Cromwell decided it was not worth garrisoning, and in 1691 part was blown up and thereafter it was used as a quarry by local farmers.

Glossary

Barbican   Outwork defending a castle's entrance.

Barmkin   Enclosing wall (esp. surrounding a tower house).

Bartizan   Corbelled turret, round or square, at the top angle of the wall-head.

Bastion   Projecting towers from a curtain wall.

Battlement   A crenellated parapet on a wall-head.

Corbel   A stone projection from the face of a wall to carry a weight.

Curtain-wall   The connecting wall between the towers of a castle.

Donjon   The keep or central fortress of a castle.

Keep   The principal tower of a castle.

Loops   Holes or slits through which arrows or guns could be fired.

Machicolation   A series of openings in the floor of a projecting gallery allowing defenders to attack besiegers from above.

Motte   A mound of earth, surrounded by a wooden tower or palisade, in turn surrounded by a ditch. Often these castles had a further palisade and ditch below, enclosing domestic buildings. This was called the "bailey".

Pleasance   A walled garden.

Rampart   A flat-topped defensive mound.

Slighting   The dismantling of the defences of a castle, to prevent an enemy making use of it.